how2become

A London Taxi Driver

Visit www.wizann.co.uk for professional
London Taxi Driver Knowledge training
courses and support

Orders: Please contact How2become Ltd, Suite 2, 50 Churchill Square Business Centre, Kings Hill, Kent ME19 4YU. Telephone: (44) 0845 643 1299 — Lines are open Monday to Friday 9am until 5pm. Fax: (44) 01732 525965. You can also order via the e-mail address info@how2become.co.uk

ISBN: 978-1-907558-31-3

First published 2013

Typeset for How2become Ltd by Molly Hill, Canada.

Printed in Great Britain for How2become Ltd by Bell & Bain Ltd, 303 Burnfield Road, Thornliebank, Glasgow G46 7UQ.

CONTENTS

CONTENTS

Dear Sir/Madam,

Welcome to your new 'How to become a London Taxi Cab Driver' information guide. Thank you for your custom.

As a London taxi cab driver you will be joining an elite club of the world's most respected taxi drivers. Also known as the London Black Cab, these vehicles and their drivers have earned the reputation for providing the best taxi service in the world. Every driver is required to undergo a rigorous test of his/her knowledge of London which can take up to four years to learn before the coveted badge is awarded. Each individual's character is tested and checks are made regarding any criminal records.

This guide has been split up into numerous sections to help you concentrate on specific areas whilst learning the 'knowledge'. You will find the guide relatively easy to use.

As part of your package we have provided you with free access to Blue Books Runs and resources. You can get access to these documents at the following website:

http://www.taxidrivercourse.co.uk

Your journey to becoming a London Taxi Cab Driver starts here. Whilst the road is a long one, excuse the pun, it will be your patience, persistence and determination that will see you through to the end.

Good luck and best wishes,

The How2become team

INTRODUCTION
ABOUT THE KNOWLEDGE

Before we start teaching you how to become a London taxi driver it is important to provide you with some basic information about the Knowledge and its history.

The history of the knowledge dates back many years to the Twelfth Century when the right to ply for hire was first given to the watermen of the river Thames by Royal Charter.

Back in the Twelfth Century it was only royal palaces very large, posh buildings and mansions that spread the front of the river Thames. In addition to these fantastic buildings were famous landmarks such as the Tower of London, palace of Westminster, Lambeth Palace, Richmond Palace, Hampton Court and Windsor Castle.

It was in1625 when the first 'transportation' began to ply for trade in the form of four wheeled coaches. The first ever

 how2become

Hackney cab stand appeared at the Maypole in the Strand during the same year. This is where Captain Baily, who was said to have accompanied Raleigh in his last expedition to Guiana, employed four hackney coaches, with drivers in liveries, to ply for hire, fixing his own rates.

It was these coaches that the name 'Hackney Coaches' was derived from and from then on in all coaches for hire became known as this. By the year 1636 there were 50 Hackney carriages by proclamation of King Charles I.

By the year 1694, under the Cromwell government, 250 Hackney coaches were licensed to ply for hire in London. In 1679 the conditions of fitness for Hackney coaches was laid down — every coach shall be 10 foot long the coach shall be strong and able to carry four persons at least. No horse shall be under 14 hands in size and they must be fit and strong. As the city grew so did the number of hackneys and by 1831 there were 1,200!

It was in the month of December, 1834, when Joseph Aloysious Hansom registered his Patent safety cab entitled 'Hansom'. Hansom eventually sold his rights in the cab for £10,000. Hansom's name was mistaken for the most famous London cab of all. This was a two wheeler Hansom cab which incorporated a driver at the rear. This cab was the invention of a man called John Chapman. The new owners of the Hansom cab company quickly brought Chapman's patent, and within a few months had 50 of these cabs working the London streets.

It wasn't until 1903 that the first petrol driven cabs were introduced onto the roads and streets of London. There were, however, the famous battery operated 'humming bird' cabs which came as early as 1897, hence called due to their quiet 'humming' noise. The major problem with the humming bird

cab was that they were so quiet nobody could hear them coming and as a result they were likely to cause accidents!

During 1905 in Vauxhall, the Vauxhall Motor Company brought out a similar cab to the Hansom with the driver at the rear, without a horse, using 7-9 hp.

In 1869 control of the cabs was given to the Home Secretary who delegated his authority to the Commissioner of police, who in turn set up The Public Carriage Office, and because of these stringent arrangements London has the finest taxi service in the world.

The 1950's saw the Austin FX3 the father of the FX4 and grandfather of the TX1TX11.

Wilhelm Bruhn invented the taximeter in 1891, and it is from the word taximeter that taxi became the new word for the cab. The taximeter measured the distance as well as the time taken for an accurate fare of the journey to be charged. The word comes from French *taxe* ('price') and Greek *metron* ('measure'). It was disliked by cab drivers who did not want to be told the fares to charge by machines.

There were reports that Wilhelm Bruhn ended up being thrown in the river Thames by angry cab drivers, although the word taxi and taximeters were here to stay and are now in use worldwide.

As a licensed taxi driver in the London Capital you must have a detailed knowledge of roads and places of interest in London — this is known as the Knowledge.

How long it takes to become a licensed taxi driver in London will very much depend on whether you want to be an 'All London' driver or a Suburban driver. There are varying different requirements for each. All London drivers, also

known as 'Green Badge' drivers, need a detailed knowledge of London within a six mile radius of Charing Cross.

To begin with there are 320 routes or 'runs' to learn, along with all the places of interest and important landmarks on and around these runs. It takes between two to four years to learn and pass the 'All London' Knowledge and this takes a considerable amount of commitment and dedication.

Once you are licensed you can work anywhere in the Greater London area and the benefits of this are huge! To obtain copies of the blue book runs please go to your resource suite at:

http://www.taxidrivercourse.co.uk

WHAT IS 'THE KNOWLEDGE'?

The taxicab driver is required to be able to decide routes immediately in response to a passenger's request or traffic conditions, rather than stopping to look at a map or ask a controller by radio.

Consequently, the Knowledge is the in-depth study of London street routes and places of interest that taxicab-drivers in that city must complete to obtain a licence to operate a black cab. It was initiated in 1865, and has changed little since.

It is the world's most demanding training course for taxicab-drivers; and applicants will usually need at least 12 'Appearances' (attempts at the final test), after preparation averaging 34 months, to pass the examination.

COURSE DETAILS

The 320 main (standard) routes, or 'runs', through central London of the Knowledge are contained within the 'Blue Book' (officially known as the 'Guide to Learning the Knowledge of London'), produced by the Public Carriage Office which regulates licensed taxis in London. In all some 25,000 streets within a six mile radius of Charing Cross are covered along with the major arterial routes through the rest of London.

A taxicab-driver must learn these, as well as the 'points of interest' along those routes including streets, squares, clubs, hospitals, hotels, theatres, government and public buildings, railway stations, police stations, courts, diplomatic buildings, important places of worship, cemeteries, crematoria, parks and open spaces, sports and leisure centres, places of learning, restaurants and historic buildings.

The Knowledge includes such details as the order of theatres on Shaftesbury Avenue, or the names and order of the side streets and traffic signals passed on a route. There are separate shorter courses, for suburban London, with 30 to 50 'runs' depending on the sector.

"KNOWLEDGE BOYS"

During training would-be cabbies, known as Knowledge boys (or girls), usually follow these routes around London on a motor scooter, and can be identified by the clipboard fixed to the handlebars and showing details of the streets to be learned that day.

In order to pass the Knowledge applicants must have a clean driving licence and no criminal record. They also need to pass a written test, which then qualifies them to make an

'appearance'.

At appearances, Knowledge boys must, without looking at a map, identify the quickest and most sensible route between any two points in metropolitan London that their examiner chooses. For each route, the applicants must recite the names of the roads used, when they cross junctions, use roundabouts, make turns, and what is 'alongside' them at each point.

Let's now take a look at the minimum eligibility requirements for becoming a London taxi dirver.

CHAPTER ONE
MINIMUM ELIGIBILITY REQUIREMENTS

In order to apply for a license you will need to satisfy the following five basic requirements:

- You have to be old enough

- To be of good character

- To be fit, both physically and mental

- To be able to drive a taxi competently and safely

- To have a thorough knowledge of London

Whilst the first 4 requirements are relatively easy to meet, the final one 'a thorough knowledge of London' is undoubtedly the toughest and one that takes dedication and hard work!

AGE LIMIT

By law you cannot hold a taxi cab driver's licence until you are 21 years of age.

There is no upper age limit at this present time and, providing you meet all of the relevant criteria, then you can be issued with a taxi cab driver's licence.

YOUR CHARACTER

Every applicant is the subject of a criminal record check before being issued with a cab driver's licence. If you have had any convictions, then you are advised to disclose all of them on your application form. A conviction does not necessarily preclude you from holding a licence. However, it does depend on what the conviction was for, and the sentence imposed.

You can learn more about the vetting process in your online resources area here:

http://www.taxidrivercourse.co.uk

It is essential that you disclose all convictions and any charges or summonses that you have pending. Failure to disclose current convictions is likely to result in the refusal of your application.

YOUR FITNESS

Every applicant who applies to become a London taxi cab driver is required to have a medical examination. This is issued by the Public Carriage Office and must be completed by your GP or other qualified doctor.

The medical report essentially covers seven major areas. These are:

- Cardiovascular i.e. heart
- Endocrine system i.e. diabetes
- Epilepsy
- Nervous system (including progressive illnesses)
- Psychiatric illness
- Vision
- Musculoskeletal i.e. body

The following medical conditions may prevent you from holding a taxi cab driver's licence.

- Epilepsy
- Insulin dependent diabetes
- Monocular vision or poor vision either with our without glasses.
- A progressive illness
- History of alcohol or drug abuse
- Physical disability which might impair the ability to drive a taxi safely or assist disabled/wheelchair passengers
- Heart problems (e.g. heart attack, heart surgery)
- Neurological or neurosurgical disorders (e.g. strokes, blackouts, head injuries) Certain prescribed medications

A THOROUGH KNOWLEDGE OF LONDON (THE KNOWLEDGE)

In order to become a London taxi cab driver you must have a thorough knowledge of London. This includes the location of streets, squares, clubs, hospitals, hotels, theatres, government and public buildings, railway stations, police stations, courts, diplomatic buildings, important places of worship, cemeteries, crematoria, parks and open spaces, sports and leisure centres, places of learning, restaurants and historic buildings; in fact everything you need to know to be able to take passengers to their destinations by the most direct routes.

You may be licensed either for the whole of London or for one or more of the 9 suburban sectors.

The "All London" licence requires you to have a detailed knowledge of the 25,000 streets within a six mile radius of Charing Cross with a more general knowledge of the major arterial routes throughout the rest of London.

If you wish to work as a taxi driver in central London or at Heathrow Airport you need an "All London" licence.

Alternatively, you may choose to study for a suburban licence. Outside the six mile radius London is divided into 9 sectors. You can select one of these and will be required to have a detailed knowledge of your chosen sector along with a more general knowledge of Central London. You may add additional sectors once licensed if you so wish.

KNOWLEDGE ASSESSMENT

Assessment is by means of an initial written test which determines whether you have reached the required standard to commence "appearances."

Appearances are a number of one to one oral examinations conducted by a qualified Knowledge of London Examiner. The examiner grades each applicant according to his or her performance. The higher the grade on each appearance, the quicker the applicant can expect to receive a licence.

Some applicants pass the Knowledge with as few as 10 or 12 appearances while others take longer.

THE DRIVING TEST

As a London taxi cab driver you will be carrying passengers for hire and reward in a purpose built vehicle which has different driving characteristics from a standard car. Therefore, you will need to take a taxi driving test so that the Licensing Authority can be assured as to your level of competence when driving the vehicle safely in a congested city environment. During the test you will also be assessed on your ability to use the facilities provided to assist the disabled i.e. wheelchair facilities and a swivel seat.

The test is conducted by a member of the Public Carriage Office staff who is trained to assess and examine the tests.

If you are physically handicapped you can still become a taxi driver providing you are able to pass the driving test. If necessary, you will be permitted to use a cab which has been modified to approved standards, to cater for your particular disability.

CHAPTER TWO

THE DIFFERENT STAGES TO BECOMING A LONDON TAXI DRIVER

INTRODUCTION

Before being licensed as a London taxi driver you will have to demonstrate that you are able to take passengers to their destination by the shortest possible route. To do this you must first learn the 'Knowledge of London' and then pass a series of examinations at London Taxi and Private Hire (LTPH).

There are two types of London taxi driver:

- **All London** – allowed to ply for hire anywhere in Greater London

- **Suburban** – allowed to ply for hire in restricted areas in the suburbs

Both All London and Suburban applicants have to demonstrate a detailed knowledge of their chosen area and the following paragraphs describe in detail the examination system and explain how you progress through it. The description is supplemented by the flowchart at Appendix A.

The nine suburban sectors are:

- Enfield, Haringey and Waltham Forest
- Barking & Dagenham
- Havering
- Newham and Redbridge Bexley
- Greenwich and Lewisham
- Bromley
- Croydon
- Merton and Sutton
- Hounslow
- Kingston upon Thames and Richmond upon Thames
- Ealing and Hillingdon
- Barnet
- Brent and Harrow

STAGE 1 — INTRODUCTORY PACK

Following satisfactory character and medical checks, you will be sent a Knowledge of London introductory pack.

The pack will include:

- a copy of 'The Guide to learning the Knowledge of London' (commonly known as the 'Blue Book');

- a booklet explaining how to learn the Knowledge, and KoL Exam System

- a copy of the DVD 'Go Your Own Way' which provides further useful information to help you through the learning and testing process.

Annex A of the All London Blue Book lists 320 routes within the six mile radius of Charing Cross; the number of routes for each Suburban sector varies according to the size of the sector. These routes will provide the basis of what you will need to learn.

STAGE 1A — SELF ASSESSMENT (ALL LONDON APPLICANTS ONLY)

The self-assessment, based on the first 80 runs in the Blue Book, is designed to let you know whether you are doing things the right way. Better to find out at this stage than after you have spent many months doing it wrong! It allows you to check that you are learning the Knowledge in the right way and to the proper standard.

The assessment takes the same form as the written examination described in Stage 2. After you have taken the assessment you will be shown the answers and you will mark your own paper. A Knowledge Examiner will be

present and will talk you through the answers and deal with any queries you may have. You don't have to tell anyone how well (or badly!) you got on. You should be left with a fuller understanding of what is required when learning the Knowledge of London and the nature of the Stage 2 Written Examination. Taking the self-assessment is optional and no record of the result is made.

The self-assessment is normally undertaken within 6 months of starting the Knowledge.

WRITTEN EXAMINATION (ALL LONDON APPLICANTS ONLY)

The written examination consists of two sections.

This section will test your knowledge of the routes in the Blue Book. You will be presented with three possible routes and be required to identify the one that gives the shortest possible route between the start and finish points. There are five questions of this nature. Each correct answer is worth 10 marks, so a total of 50 marks are available for the section.

This section will test your knowledge of points that you should have encountered when learning the Blue Book runs.

You will be presented with a list of 25 points and for each one you will be given four possible locations. You have to identify the correct one. Each correctly identified point is worth two marks so a total of 50 marks are available for this section. The total mark for the two sections is 100. The pass mark is 60%.

If you are successful you progress to Stage 3 of the selection process. If you fail to achieve the pass mark you can apply to re-sit the written examination at a later date. However, the score you achieve and the number of times you have sat the

exam will determine how long you will be required to wait before being able to re-sit the written examination.

The Stage 2 written examination has to be undertaken within 24 months of being sent your introductory pack. A fee is payable for each written examination you take. You can find the current fee on the Taxi and Private Hire pages of the TfL website.

STAGES 3 TO 5 — APPEARANCES (GENERAL INFORMATION)

There are three stages of one-to-one oral examinations, known as appearances. In each of Stages 3, 4 and 5 you are likely to have to take several examinations.

As you progress from one stage to another the intervals between examinations will become shorter. Initially, examinations will be eight weeks apart, reducing to three weeks at the advanced stage. A one-off fee is payable when you start appearances. The current fee can be found on the Taxi and Private Hire pages of the TfL website.

All appearances are conducted by Knowledge of London Examiners. In the interests of fairness, you will be examined by different examiners in rotation.

Therefore, during the appearance stages you will be seen by a variety of examiners. Your first appearance will last approximately 30 minutes. Subsequent appearances will last up to 20 minutes. Each examination will involve the examiner asking you to state the location of two specified points of interest. This can be a street, a square, etc. or a named building, in other words anywhere that a taxi passenger might ask to be taken.

If you can give the correct locations of the two points you will be asked to describe the shortest possible route between the two.

During the course of one examination you will be asked four questions of this nature. At any point in Stages 3, 4 and 5 the examiner may ask questions that focus on areas where you appear to have had difficulty in previous appearances.

The examination system is designed to allow you the opportunity to prove that you have the necessary knowledge to give a good service as a taxi driver.

However, whilst there is no intention to cause unnecessary pressure or catch you out, as you progress through the appearances stages not only will you have to demonstrate a higher level of Knowledge but the precision and fluency of your answers will be expected to improve.

APPEARANCES MARKING SYSTEM

The same marking system is used for Stages 3, 4 and 5.

There will be a maximum of 10 marks available for each question giving a potential maximum of 40 for the examination. You will be asked to identify the start and finish points of a run. If you fail to identify the location of a point you will be asked an alternative but you will be deducted one mark for each point you fail to identify.

Once you have successfully located the start and finish points you will be asked to describe the route between the two. Your answer will be scored out of the number of marks remaining from the original 10. You will lose marks if, for example:

- you give incorrect street names;

- the route is not the most direct available;

- the route involves making banned turns or U-turns, contravening 'no entry' signs or travelling the wrong way down one-way streets;

- you show such hesitancy in delivering the answer that may indicate that you cannot recall the route quickly enough to be able to drive confidently and safely in London traffic.

Therefore, if you correctly identify the first start and finish points you are asked and call the run perfectly you will be awarded 10 marks for that question. Conversely, if you fail to identify 10 points the run cannot be attempted and no marks can be awarded.

If when calling a run, you make an illegal manoeuvre e.g. calling a banned turn, contravening a one-way street, etc. then you will receive no marks for that question. The total number of marks scored over the four questions is translated into an overall grade for the appearance. Five grades can be awarded. The grades are then translated into points, which, when accumulated in each stage of appearances, will allow you to progress to the next stage.

40	Grade AA	12 points	Exceptional
36-39	Grade A	6 points	Very good
32-35	Grade B	4 points	Good
24-31	Grade C	3 points	Satisfactory
<24	Grade D	0 points	Unsatisfactory

The total number of points needed to progress to the next stage is 12. If you accumulate four D grades on any stage

you have to re-start the stage, regardless of the number of points already gained in that stage. If on the second attempt at the stage you again accumulate four D grades you will go back to the beginning of the previous stage (see diagram at Appendix A).

The examiners are allowed to award one U (for untested) grade per stage, this can take account of a performance that has been affected by illness, domestic problems, etc., treating each case on merit. A U grade does not affect your progress through the stage.

STAGE 3 APPEARANCES — BASIC POINTS AND RUNS

The questions in your first appearance at Stage 3 will be based on routes listed in Annex B of the Blue Book, although the start and finish points of some questions will be varied to include places of interest either on the route or within the ¼ or ½ mile radius of either end. In subsequent appearances the questions may not necessarily be based on routes listed in the Blue Book.

You will be asked prominent points at these appearances such as major hotels, railway stations, magistrates' and crown courts, etc.

If you realise that you have made a mistake when calling a run, you will be allowed to go back and correct any errors without being penalised for doing so. When you have gained 12 points you will progress to Stage 4. Stage 3 appearances are approximately 56 days apart

STAGE 4 APPEARANCES — INTERMEDIATE POINTS AND RUNS

The start and finish points specified will again be places of interest on or within the ¼ or ½ mile radius of either end of Blue Book routes, but both points of any one question will not be from the same Blue Book route. These questions are designed to allow you to show that you can link and combine Blue Book routes, enabling you to prove you can cope with more complex routes.

At this stage you will not be permitted to correct errors when calling a run. When you have gained 12 points you will progress to Stage 5. Stage 4 appearances are approximately 28 days apart

STAGE 5 APPEARANCES — ADVANCED POINTS AND RUNS

This is the final one-to-one examination stage covering the central six-mile radius area or your chosen sector. The questions will no longer be linked to the routes at Annex B of the Blue Book and the examiner will ask questions that allow you to demonstrate that you have the necessary knowledge to take a passenger to any location in your licence area.

At this stage you will have to prove that your Knowledge is up to date and topical e.g. awareness of new tourist attractions, current theatre productions, changes in hotel names, high profile temporary events such as Chelsea Flower Show, Christmas ice rinks, etc.

At this stage, Suburban applicants may be asked questions about major locations in the adjoining sectors. This will be limited to large points such as transport hubs, 5 star hotels, sports venues, hospitals, etc. On gaining the required 12

points you will progress to Stage 6. Stage 5 appearances are approximately 21 days apart.

STAGE 6 APPEARANCE — SUBURBAN/INNER LONDON EXAMINATION

This stage is a single one-to-one examination held six weeks after your final Stage 5 appearance.

On completing Stage 5, All London applicants will be required to learn the 25 suburban routes listed in Annex C of the Blue Book prior to the Stage 6 examination. Of these routes 21 radiate from the edge of the six-mile radius to the outskirts of Greater London and four from London Heathrow Airport. The questions in the examination will be based on these routes.

For suburban applicants the questions are based on a list, issued to you at the end of Stage 5, of places you are required to know in central London (e.g. hospitals, railway termini, etc.). You must be able to tell the examiner the route from your sector to such places. You must also know the routes from your sector to London Heathrow and London City Airports.

If you are unsuccessful you can attend for re-examination after an interval of approximately 2 weeks.

STAGE 7 — FINAL TALK AND PRESENTATION OF TAXI DRIVER'S LICENCE AND BADGE

When you have passed the Stage 6 examination (and as long as you have met all the other requirements for licensing i.e. character, medical checks, taxi driving test) you can make the final application for the issue of your licence. You will need

to show us your driving licence and pay the fee for the issue of a taxi driver's licence. You can find the current fee on the TfL website. You will then be invited to return to LTPH for the presentation of your licence and badge. You will join a group of other successful candidates to receive advice about your responsibilities as a taxi driver from a Knowledge of London Examiner. At the conclusion of the talk a TPH senior manager will present you with your licence and badge.

12. ACCESSIBILITY

The Knowledge of London examination system is able to accommodate any individual or special needs you may have through a variety of means e.g. a flexible appointments system, extended appearances if you have communication difficulties, accessible facilities for disabled candidates, etc. If you have any special needs that need to be taken into consideration during the examination process you should advise a member of LTPH.

13. COMPLAINTS AND APPEALS

If at any time during the examination process you have a complaint or a query regarding your examinations you should contact the Knowledge of London Manager. All complaints and appeals are treated in confidence and will not have any adverse effect on your progress through the examination system.

APPENDIX A – KNOWLEDGE OF LONDON EXAMINATION SYSTEM FLOWCHART

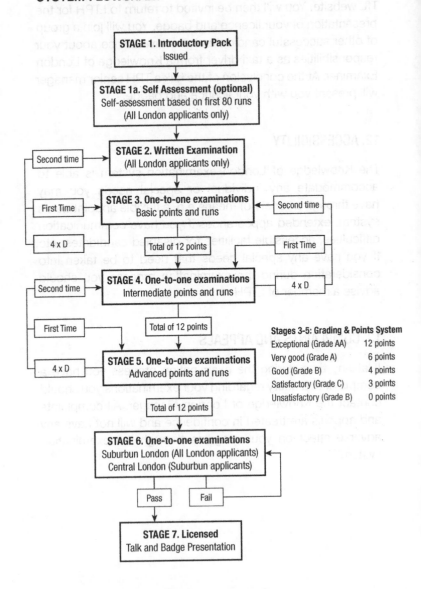

STAGE 1. Introductory Pack
Issued

STAGE 1a. Self Assessment (optional)
Self-assessment based on first 80 runs
(All London applicants only)

STAGE 2. Written Examination
(All London applicants only)

Second time

STAGE 3. One-to-one examinations
Basic points and runs

First Time

4 x D

Total of 12 points

Second time

First Time

STAGE 4. One-to-one examinations
Intermediate points and runs

Second time

4 x D

Total of 12 points

First Time

4 x D

STAGE 5. One-to-one examinations
Advanced points and runs

Stages 3-5: Grading & Points System
Exceptional (Grade AA)   12 points
Very good (Grade A)   6 points
Good (Grade B)   4 points
Satisfactory (Grade C)   3 points
Unsatisfactory (Grade B)   0 points

Total of 12 points

STAGE 6. One-to-one examinations
Suburbun London (All London applicants)
Central London (Suburbun applicants)

Pass   Fail

STAGE 7. Licensed
Talk and Badge Presentation

APPENDIX B – WRITTEN EXAMINATION FLOWCHART

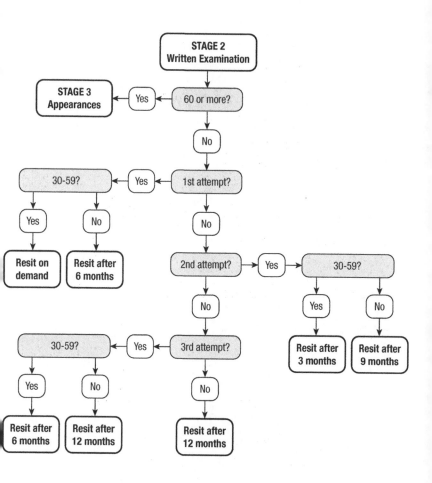

APPENDIX B — WRITTEN EXAMINATION FLOWCHART

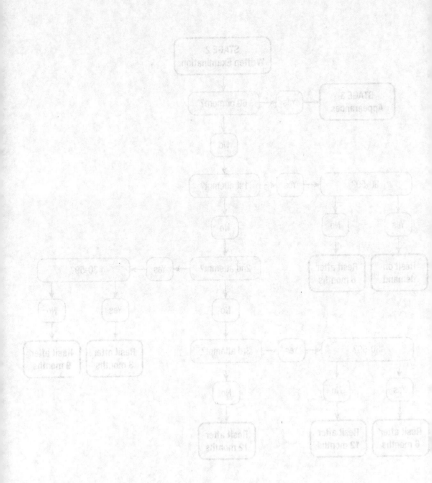

CHAPTER THREE

MAKING YOUR APPLICATION

THE APPLICATION PACK

The first step in becoming a licensed London Taxi Driver is to obtain an application pack. The easiest way to obtain your application pack is by registering your details on line at the following website:

http://www.tfl.gov.uk

To go direct to the application form page, please log in to your resource suite at:

http://www.taxidrivercourse.co.uk

Once you are at the relevant application page, all you need to do is complete each of the boxes marked with a mandatory field asterix (*) and submit the form.

Application packs usually arrive within 2-3 days but please allow up to 10 days maximum for the pack to arrive.

If you do not have access to a PC or the internet then you can obtain an application pack by writing to the following address or by telephone, fax and e-mail:

London Taxi and Private Hire
Palestra
4th Floor Green Zone
197 Blackfriars Road
London
SE1 8NJ
Telephone — 0845 602 7000
Email — TPH.Enquiries@tfl.gov.uk

COMPLETING THE APPLICATION

Step 1

The first step, before putting pen to paper, is to read every part of the application pack. This will give you a full understanding of what is required in order to complete the form correctly which will in turn reduce the application time and thus make the process far smoother.

The forms you must read fully are as follows:

MHC/201 — A reference guide to becoming a taxi driver Guidance notes to the Enhanced CRB Disclosure form Disclosure application form

MHC/203 — London Taxi Driver Licensing Application Form

MHC/207 — Fees and Additional costs

MHC/210 — Equal Opportunities Monitoring Form

MHC/211 — Information for applicants (Suburban Taxi Drivers)

TPH/204 – Medical Declaration

Step 2

Once you have read every part of the application pack it is now time to complete the form which is entitled MHC/203 'London Taxi Driver Licence Application Form'.

Step 3

Complete the Criminal Records Bureau Disclosure application form

Step 4

Provide the relevant forms of identification. Details of what is required are provided in the guidance notes.

Step 5

You now need to submit your application. This can only be done in person by attending the Public Carriage Office at the following address:

London Taxi and Private Hire
Palestra
4th Floor Green Zone
197 Blackfriars Road
London
SE1 8NJ

Opening hours for the PCO are as follows:

Monday to Friday between 8am and 4pm (except Bank Holidays)

Before you go to the PCO to submit your application make

sure you take the following with you:

- Completed application form (MHC/203).

- Completed CRB Disclosure application form which is done online.

- Your driving licence and all of the relevant forms of ID (see guidance notes in your application pack).

- Payment to cover the licence application fee and the CRB Disclosure application fee.

- You will also need a pre-addressed envelope and a TMG CRB introductory letter.

Once you have submitted your application the PCO will immediately provide you with a medical examination form, providing you have not declared any convictions. If you do declare any convictions then you will have to wait for the CRB check to be carried out before being issued with your medical form.

Step 6 — The medical examination

Once you have received your medical examination form it is vital that you visit your GP (or other doctor) to undergo the examination as soon as possible. You only have 28 days in which to submit your completed application form so don't delay!

If the form is not submitted within 28 days then your application will proceed no further.

Once you have satisfied all of the requirements, including the CRB check (if applicable) and the medical examination then you can proceed to the 'Knowledge' stage of the selection process.

CHAPTER FOUR

HOW TO TACKLE THE BLUE BOOK RUNS

The List of Routes issued to knowledge students by the PCO is more commonly known as "Blue Book Runs". The routes are simply a list of journeys ie:

- Manor House Station, N4 to Gibson Square, N1
- Thornhill Square, N1 to Queen Square, WC1
- Chancery Lane Station, WC1 to Rolls Road, SE1

There are 320 runs in total and they are the foundation for the knowledge of London. You must be aware that the list of Blue Book routes is just a guide. For this reason, knowing the right way to learn your Blue Book Runs is very important.

To obtain copies of the Blue Book please log in to your resource suite here:

http://www.taxidrivercourse.co.uk

An examiner will not usually ask you runs as they are outlined within the book, but runs which NEARLY CORRESPOND to those routes.

For example, he will not ask you to take him from Manor House Station to Gibson Square (List 1, No. 1) because you could have memorised the route from a computer, map or printed route without ever having undertaken the journey. Instead you could be asked John Scott Health Centre (near Manor House Station) to Almedia Theatre (near Gibson Square). Your ability to answer will establish that you have completed the journey and, more importantly, that you have familiarised yourself with the area around the destination and departure point.

The examiner may want to go from any of the points in Circle A to any of the points in Circle B on a map. The route between the circles always remains basically the same. You must be aware of the importance of alternative points because if you do not know the starting point or the finishing point selected by the examiner, then you cannot answer, even though you may know the basic route.

Failure to achieve this will mean that you will have to cover all the same ground again to collect points you could have seen first time. Once you have learned the value of knowing points at the start and end of each route, what about points along the route? Do not try to learn these at the same time; it is too much to absorb all at once and will only lead to confusion. These points take care of themselves at a later date.

Let us show you how. If we now add other runs that you will encounter later in the Blue Book you will see how you learn points naturally between the beginning and end of the journey from point A to point B, thus, acting as revision for parts of a previous route.

Gradually you will see how the quarter mile radius falls into place like pieces of a jigsaw puzzle, constantly building your topographical "Knowledge".

Remember, the important thing is to get a mental picture of the map in your head, so that when you do call-over practice or attempt to answer the examiner's questions you should have a visual image in your mind's eye of the route and the points at the beginning and end.

It is easy to be tempted into racing through the "Blue Book", doing as many runs as possible, but in the long term you will get through the knowledge quicker if you concentrate on the quality of your learning rather than the quantity.

"Calling-over" (revising runs by repeatedly reciting them) is very important, as it is the only way possible to see how well you are remembering the journeys you have already made. When you call basic "Blue Book" almost anybody can assist you and you should do this as often you can, but what you should be doing is moving toward calling alternative point to alternative point as soon as possible.

Before we show you how to calculate a route, take a look at 6 sample blue book runs on the following pages.

LIST 1 RUN 1
Manor House Stn (N4) to Gibson Sq (N1)

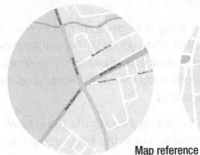 

Map reference

Collins - Knowledge Map **27**-N2   Collins — Knowledge Map **27**-L10

Collins - Street Atlas **75**-J7   Collins — Street Atlas **111**-G1

Lve on L	Green Lanes — *T & G.W.U. on L*
R&R	Highbury New Park
L	Highbury Grove
R	Saint Pauls Rd — *Alwyne Castle PH on L*
Comply	Highbury Corner
Lve by	Upper St — *Islington Museum on L*
R	Barnsbury St
L	Milner Square
F	Milner Place
F into	Gibson Square

Reverse Friendly

Run Length 4.4 KM

LIST 1 RUN 2
Thornhill Sq (N1) to Queen Sq (WC1)

Map reference

Collins - Knowledge Map **27**-K9   Collins — Knowledge Map **39**-J4
Collins - Street Atlas **93**-F7   Collins — Street Atlas **10**-B7

Lve by	Matilda St
R	Copenhagen St
L	Caledonian Rd
L	Carnegie St
R	Muriel St
F	Rodney St — *Joe Grimaldi Pk on R*
F	Penton Rise — *Paul Robeson Hse on L*
F	King's Cross Rd — *Thistle Kings X on L*
R	Acton St
L	Grays Inn Rd
R	Guilford St — *Grenville Hse Hotel on L*
L	Guilford Place
F	Lamb's Conduit St
R	Great Ormond St
F into	Queen Square

Run Length 2.8 KM

LIST 1 RUN 3
Chancery Lane Stn (WC1) to Rolls Rd (SE1)

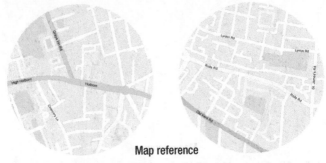

Map reference

Collins - Knowledge Map *39*-L4	Collins - Knowledge Map *51*-R1
Collins - Street Atlas *19*-E2	Collins - Street Atlas *37*-H3

Lve on L	High Holborn
F	Holborn *Ryl Fusiliers Mem. on R*
Comply	Holborn Circus
Lve by	St. Andrew St *Ryl Col. of Organists on L*
F	Shoe Lane
L	Stonecutter St
R	Farringdon St
F	Ludgate Circus
F	New Bridge St *Blackfriars PH on L*
F	Blackfriars Bridge
F	Blackfriars Rd *Ludgate Hse on L*
L	Southwark St
R	Southwark Bridge Rd
L	Marshalsea Rd
F	Great Dover St
Comply	Bricklayer's Arms
Lve by	Old Kent Rd
L	Rowcross St
L or R	Rolls Rd

Run Length 5.0 KM

LIST 1 RUN 4
Pages Walk (SE1) to St. Martin's Theatre (WC2)

Map reference

Collins - Knowledge Map **27**-K9   Collins — Knowledge Map **39**-J4
Collins - Street Atlas **93**-F7   Collins — Street Atlas **10**-B7

Lve on L	Grange Rd
F	Bermondsey St
L	Long Lane
R	Great Dover St
L	Borough High St
R	Lant St
L	Toulmin St
R	Great Suffolk St
L	Webber St — *Old Vic Stage Door on L*
L	The Cut
R	Waterloo Rd
Comply	Tenison Way
Lve by	Waterloo Bridge
F	Lancaster Pl
F	Aldwych — *No.1 Aldwych Hotel on L*
L	Catherine St
L	Exeter St
R	Wellington St — *Orso Restaurant on L*
F	Bow St
Comply	Roundabout
Lve by	Endell St
L	Shelton St — *Urdang Academy on L*
R	Mercer St
Comply	Seven Dials
Lve by	Earlham St
L	Shaftesbury Ave
L	West St

SDOL

Run Length 4.8 KM

LIST 1 RUN 5
Australia House (WC2) to Paddington Station (W2)

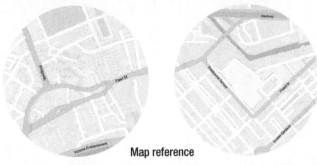

Map reference

Collins - Knowledge Map *39*-K5   Collins — Knowledge Map *38*-B5
Collins - Street Atlas *18*-D4   Collins — Street Atlas *14*-E3

Lve on R	Strand
R	Aldwych — *Waldorf Hotel on L*
L	Drury Lane — *Sorastro Restnt. on R*
L	High Holborn — *Oasis Leisure on L*
F	Princes Circus
Lve by	St Giles High St
R	Earnshaw St
L	New Oxford St
F	St Giles Circus
F	Oxford St — *M&S Pantheon on L*
F	Oxford Circus
F	Oxford St
R	Portman Street
L	Seymour Street
R	Edgware Road
L	Harrow Road
Comply	Harrow Road Circus
Lve by	Bishops Bridge Road
L	Eastbourne Terrace
L	Departures Rd

WARNING: Oxford St is access for Buses and Taxis Only. The failure to take note of road signs can lead to penalty points.

S.D.O.L.

Run Length 5.5 KM

LIST 1 RUN 6
Lancaster Gate (W2) to Royal Free Hospital (NW3)

Map reference

Collins - Knowledge Map *38*-A6
Collins - Street Atlas *14*-D5

Collins — Knowledge Map *26*-C7
Collins — Street Atlas *91*-H5

Lve on L	Bayswater Rd
L	Lancaster Terrace
F+R	Sussex Gardens
L	Spring Street
F	Eastbourne Terrace
R	Bishops Bridge Road
Comply	Harrow Road Circus
Lve by	Warwick Avenue
R	Blomfield Road
L	Maida Vale
R	Saint Johns Wood Road
L & R	Grove End Rd — *Century Crt on R*
L	Finchley Rd — *Fuji Film Hse on L*
B\R	College Crescent
R	Belsize Lane
F	Ornan Rd — *Holiday Inn NW3 on R*
L	Haverstock Hill
F	Rosslyn Hill
R	Pond St
R into	Hospital Forecourt
Exit by	Rowland Hill St

Run Length 6.0 KM

CHAPTER FIVE

HOW TO CALCULATE A ROUTE

Visit www.WizAnn.co.uk for training courses and support for becoming a London taxi driver

The following is intended to give you an insight into how to calculate a route from A to B, based upon a *moving line*. It will also show why using a *straight fixed line* on the map often leads to unnecessary detours.

Having a relatively good idea of how routes are calculated enables you to improve upon your own sense of direction and to know just what it is that you are trying to achieve with any given journey.

WHAT IS A GOOD ROUTE?

Your aim is to travel from A to B by the shortest distance. There are usually several good and acceptable answers to each journey (Point to Point). Your own judgement about this is just as valid as anybody else's and should be based upon common sense.

EXAMPLE 1

Peckham Police Station to Novotel International.

The following are three different ways of getting from A to B. Two are based upon a straight fixed line calculation and one on a moving line. It is this moving line principal that will give you the best calculation and shortest route by avoiding unnecessary detours onto a line.

All three routes will be analysed to show in detail their differences in the way they have been calculated. Bold italic lettering has been used to highlight the differences between each of these journeys.

ROUTE 1
Based on moving line
Peckham Police Stn to Novotel
International

Lve on L	Peckham High St
R	Consort Rd
R	Clayton Rd
L	Peckham High St
F	Peckham Rd
F	Camberwell Ch. St
F	Camberwell Green
F	Camberwell New Rd
F	Harleyford St
F	Kennington Oval
F	Harleyford Rd
L	South Lambeth Rd
R	Parry St
R	*Bondway*
F	*Vauxhall Cross*
F	*Bridge Foot*
F	*Vauxhall Bridge*
F	*Bessborough Gdns*
F	*Vauxhall Bridge Rd*
L	*Warwick Way*
F	*Ebury Bridge*
F	*Pimlico Rd*
R	*Lower Sloane St*
L	*Turk's Row*
R	*Franklin's Row*
L	*St. Leonard's Terrace*
R	*Walpole St*
F	*Anderson St*
F	*Sloane Ave*
F	*Pelham St*
F into	*South Kensington Junction*
Lve by	*Old Brompton Rd*
R	*Glendower Place*
L	*Harrington Rd*
F+R	*Stanhope Gardens*
L	*Cromwell Rd*
F	West Cromwell Rd
F	Talgarth Rd
R	Under Flyover
R: back into	Talgarth Rd
L	Shortlands
L	Chalk Hill Rd

S.D.O.L.

ROUTE 2
Based on fixed line
Peckham Police Stn to Novotel
International

Lve on L	Peckham High St
R	Consort Rd
R	Clayton Rd
L	Peckham High St
F	Peckham Rd
F	Camberwell Ch. St
F	Camberwell Green
F	Camberwell New Rd
F	Harleyford St
F	Kennington Oval
F	Harleyford Rd
L	South Lambeth Rd
R	Parry St
R	*Bondway*
F	*Vauxhall Cross*
F	*Bridge Foot*
F	*Vauxhall Bridge*
F	*Bessborough Gdns*
F	*Vauxhall Bridge Rd*
L	*Grosvenor Rd*
F	*Chelsea Embankment*
F	*Cheyne Walk*
F	*Cremorne Rd*
F	*Ashburnham Rd*
F	*Tadema Rd*
F	*Gunter Grove*
F	*Finborough Rd*
F	*Warwick Rd*
L	West Cromwell Rd
F	Talgarth Rd
R	Under Flyover
R: back into	Talgarth Rd
L	Shortlands
L	Chalk Hill Rd

S.D.O.L.

ROUTE 3
Based on fixed line
Peckham Police Stn to Novotel
International

Lve on L	Peckham High St
R	Consort Rd
R	Clayton Rd
L	Peckham High St
F	Peckham Rd
F	Camberwell Ch. St
F	Camberwell Green
F	Camberwell New Rd
F	Harleyford St
F	Kennington Oval
F	Harleyford Rd
L	South Lambeth Rd
R	Parry St
F	*Nine Elms Lane*
F	*Battersea Park Rd*
R	*Prince of Wales Drive*
Comply	*Queens Circus*
Lve by	*Queenstown Rd*
F	*Chelsea Bridge*
L	*Chelsea Embankment*
F	*Cheyne Walk*
F	*Cremorne Rd*
F	*Ashburnham Rd*
F	*Tadema Rd*
F	*Gunter Grove*
F	*Finborough Rd*
F	*Warwick Rd*
L	West Cromwell Rd
F	Talgarth Rd
R	Under Flyover
R: back into	Talgarth Rd
L	Shortlands
L	Chalk Hill Rd

S.D.O.L.

More roads will not necessarily mean a longer distance.

To begin to calculate your route you need to take a line from Point A to Point B. A line from Peckham Police Station to Novotel International would look something like the drawing below and travel straight through Chelsea Bridge. This is a **rough guide** line to the direction of your journey.

Because of the few options available you will see that the first part of the journey is preordained. All three routes will be the same as below until Parry St!

Lve on L	Peckham High St
R	Consort Rd
R	Clayton Rd
L	Peckham High St
F	Peckham Rd
F	Camberwell Ch. St
F	Camberwell Green
F	Camberwell New Rd
F	Harleyford St
F	Kennington Oval
F	Harleyford Rd
L	South Lambeth Rd
R	Parry St

It is only once you reach Parry St that a Question should arise. Should you head to Chelsea Bridge and cross as the fixed line suggests, or cross at Vauxhall Bridge? What you need to do is take a line from where your two ideas part and where they meet up. This will give a fairly accurate idea as to what is the shortest journey between these two points.

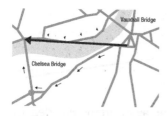

As you can see using Chelsea Bridge between these two points will be the longer journey. It is quite literally the wrong way. You would have detoured and added unnecessary distance.

If you have been given a journey from Vauxhall Bridge (Southside) to Chelsea Bridge (Northside) you would draw a line between these two points and rightly cross by the shortest option of Vauxhall Bridge. But if that line began back in Peckham, **the fixed line** would force you to make the same journey — crossing by Chelsea Bridge. This cannot be correct. The shortest journey between Vauxhall Bridge and Chelsea Bridge will always be the same regardless of where the line began.

If you cross Vauxhall Bridge, which you most definitely should on this journey, you must then re-evaluate from Vauxhall Bridge North side to Novotel International. Do not use the line you initially drew which started back in Peckham. It is void as soon as you move away and leave it behind.

Taking the line to the correct location is your next concern. In this instance your final destination (Novotel International) cannot be reached without first getting onto the West Cromwell Rd. This means that for best results you need to take your line from Vauxhall Bridge to The Junction of West Cromwell Rd & Warwick Rd.

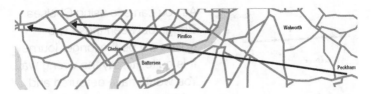

This tweaks the run even further away from the idea of perhaps following the river and instead heading through Sloane Sq.

Below are the lines following the journey of the three routes given (Peckham Police Station to Novotel International). This should clearly show that if you leave your line fixed and take it to the incorrect point you will cause the journey to be longer. The Dashed line highlights the fact that the journeys in essence are only different in the respect of how they get from Vauxhall Bridge to the Junction of West Cromwell Rd and Warwick Rd. When looked at like this Route 1 should be the journey you will favour most. Route 3 is definitely wrong.

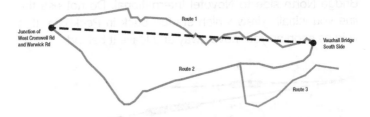

To analyse the difference between these three routes cannot be done based on a fixed line from Peckham Police Station to Novotel International. It must be done based upon the differences. All three routes reach the base of Vauxhall Bridge. The route using Chelsea Bridge is obviously wrong and can be discounted. The other two routes only differ in their journey from the north side of Vauxhall Bridge to the junction of Warwick Rd and West Cromwell Rd. It is between

these two points that you must draw a new line to evaluate the difference.

EXAMPLE 2

Cricklewood Lane to Princes Gate

Route 1

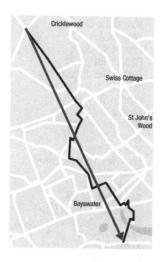

Lve on L	Cricklewood Broadway
F	Shoot Up Hill
F	Kilburn High Rd
R	Cambridge Ave
F	Cambridge Gardens
F	Rudolph Rd
R	Kilburn Park Rd
F	Kilburn Park Circus
F	Kilburn Park Rd
R	Shirland Rd
L	Chippenham Rd
L	Harrow Rd
R	Lord Hills Bridge
F	Porchester Rd
L	Bishops Bridge Rd
R	Gloucester Terrace
L	Lancaster Terrace
R	Westbourne St
L	Stanhope Terrace
R	Brook St
F	Victoria Gate
F	The {West Carriage Drive} Ring
B\R	Serpentine Rd
B\L	Serpentine Bridge
F	The {West Carriage Drive} Ring
F	Alexandra Gate
L	Kensington Rd
R into	Princes Gate

With a fixed line route 1 looks quite sensible. In reality this route is completely wrong. The fact is you must go through Victoria Gate so to take the line to Princes Gate initially will cause you to detour.

The line in route 2 has been taken to the correct location of
Victoria Gate.

Route 2

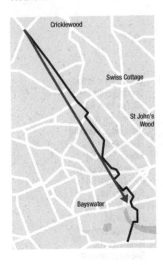

Lve on L	Cricklewood Broadway
F	Shoot Up Hill
F	Kilburn High Rd
R	Kilburn Park Rd
L	Randolph Gdns
F	Randolph Ave
R	Sutherland Ave
B\L	Warrington Cres
F	Warwick Ave
Comply	Harrow Rd Circus
Lve by	Bishops Bridge Rd
L	Eastbourne Terrace
L	Praed St
R	London St
F	Sussex Pl
R	Stanhope Terrace
L	Brook St
F	Victoria Gate
F	The {West Carriage Drive} Ring
B\R	Serpentine Rd
B\L	Serpentine Bridge
F	The {West Carriage Drive} Ring
F	Alexandra Gate
L	Kensington Rd
R into	Princes Gate

This causes you to calculate an entirely different route to that
of route 1.

CHAPTER SIX

ADVICE ON 'CALL-OVER'

WHAT IS CALL-OVER?

Call-over is the exercise of verbally reciting a run from memory that you have pre-learned. This could be a run listed in the Blue Book (Issued by the PCO) or a new route written by yourself to help with an area you personally find difficult.

Why is it important to 'Call-Over' the Blue Book runs?

Call-over gives you the ability to name roads and quickly reference a pre-set route mentally. If you stop calling over for 1 or 2 weeks you will find that the runs will begin to fade away; it then becomes very hard to get back into the habit of calling them again. The reason for this is because the runs only stay in your memory short-term. Just like the words to a song, unless you sing it regularly you won't remember it. That is why it is so important to make sure you maintain the runs by calling-over.

HOW OFTEN AND HOW MUCH SHOULD I CALL-OVER?

Call-over should be done on a day to day basis; two sessions of 30 minutes a day (basically after calling for 30 minutes you may need a break and a cup of tea).

You should reach a standard of calling at least one run per minute. If you do this daily, you will call at least 60 — 80 runs and it will only take you one hour. Calling to a time target is both motivational and good time management. The difference in the standard between someone who calls 60 runs in 4 hours and someone who calls 60 runs in 1 hour is quite simple, one will have 3 extra hours to pursue any other work they may have and the other will be very mentally drained.

Someone who calls over a lot of runs per day will 9 times out of 10 be of a higher standard than someone who only calls a few. The difference in standard between someone who calls 100 runs per a day and another who calls only 20 is enormous.

Tip: Call-Over as many runs as is possible for yourself in a 30 minute session and do this twice a day.

Tip: Time management is one of the most crucial aspects to any knowledge candidate.

Tip: If you only manage to call 10 runs in each session it is not a problem. Keeping a day-to-day record of the amounts you call will help motivate and improve upon your previous day's work.

SHOULD I CALL POINTS AT THE SAME TIME?

Revise the points at a completely separate time. If you revise the runs with the points it will only slow the whole process down.

WHAT IF I GO ON HOLIDAY?

When on holiday you should quite simply enjoy yourself, relax and to a large degree forget about the knowledge. This will allow your brain time to recoup after its onslaught of information. There is only one catch and that is you must still call-over for one hour a day, if you do not you will find yourself having to work twice as hard on your return to reach the level you were at before you left.

DO I NEED A CALL-OVER PARTNER?

Calling-over with a partner who is also doing The Knowledge is the easiest way to revise your runs. You will get feedback and encouragement from someone who very much understands the whole situation. When you read your partners runs whilst they are calling over it becomes double revision for yourself.

SHOULD MY PARTNER BE DOING THE SAME COMPANIES RUNS AS MYSELF?

Doing runs written by different people or organisations is actually an advantage. It will lead to lots of map queries and questions that will only enhance your awareness of the best route or possibilities of alternatives.

CAN I CALL-OVER ON MY OWN?

Although not ideal, it can be done and in some circumstances (depending on the individual's ability to work alone) may be even better than having a partner.

REASONS FOR WORKING ALONE:

1. You cannot find anybody living near you.
2. You do not have the time to visit someone else due to work commitments.
3. You do not like working with others.

HOW DO I CALL-OVER ALONE?

Calling over alone requires a different technique to that with a partner. When alone you should use a Dictaphone or a cassette recorder to record yourself.

Use a 30-minute cassette and it will also act as a clock for the session. Looking only at the title of the run — e.g. MANOR HOUSE STATION to GIBSON SQUARE — name all roads and turnings between the two places as fluently and consistently as possible. Continue calling routes until the cassette runs out, rewind the tape and play it back reading the runs as you go. You will hear the errors you may have made and be able to correct them there and then by calling the run again. Revising your runs by sliding your hand slowly down a page will tend to mean that you are reading rather than calling from memory – this is not advisable.

CAN I CALL-OVER WITH SOMEONE WHO IS NOT DOING THE KNOWLEDGE?

Calling-over with someone who is not doing the knowledge is not ideal but it can be done. It is most important that you explain some details to the partner to help them understand what is expected of them.

If a mistake is made, such as Street instead of Road DO NOT stop the person calling, just point out the error when the run has been called.

If you cannot remember a particular road name within a run, just ask the partner to tell you. This is not cheating it is reminding. Once told you should begin the run again, this time call the run without stopping. If you go into deep thought attempting to pull the road from memory you will just be hurting your brain and wasting time.

Never call for longer than an agreed period. If the partner knows the session will only last 20 minutes they will be far more willing to cooperate.

SHOULD I VISUALISE THE RUNS AS I CALL THEM OVER?

Visualising the runs is a completely natural learning process. It is achieved purely by the frequency upon which you travel a particular route. A good example of this will be your journey home or your journey to work, at no time did you attempt to picture these roads you travelled upon, yet I am quite sure you can clearly picture them with ease. You can do things whilst learning the runs themselves that will help with visualising, but in general it boils down to the shear amount of times you have travelled a particular road.

In the next section of your guide we have provided you with lots of sample test questions to help you get started in your preparation.

To find call over partners and advice please go to:

www.WizzAnn.co.uk

CHAPTER SEVEN
SAMPLE TEST QUESTIONS

Welcome to the London Taxi Driver Knowledge test section of your guide. You will see a range of different tests that you can use to assess your knowledge. Work through each test carefully and check your scores at the end of each test.

- Points Test (Section 1)

- Blue Book Run Test (Section 2)

- Area Points Test

- Map Test Quiz 1

- Map Test Quiz 2

- Points Test — Embassies

- Points Test — Hospitals

- Points Test — Hotels

 how2become

- Points Test — Railway Stations

- Points Test — Town Halls

- Points Test – Pubs and Bars

- Points Test – Police Stations

- Points Test – Squares

SECTION 1

Select the correct location for each of the following points by ticking the appropriate box, as shown in the example below.

Example

0. Public Carriage Office

☐ Penton Rise ☐ Penton Place ☑ Penton Street

---

1. Haig Hall

☐ New King's Rd ☐ Saint James's St ☐ Montford Place

2. 3i's House

☐ Waterloo Rd ☐ Westmister Bridge Rd ☐ Blackfriars Rd

3. Turkish Embassy

☐ Hans Crescent ☐ Chesham Place ☐ Belgrave Square

4. Abraham Lincoln Statue

☐ Parliament Square ☐ Trafalgar Square ☐ Russell Square

5. Benjy's 2000 Nightclub

☐ Clapham High St ☐ Harlesden High St ☐ Mile End Rd

6. Richmond House

☐ Putney Bridge Rd ☐ Whitehall ☐ Upper Richmond Rd

7. Prince of Wales Theatre

☐ Old Compton St ☐ Sherwood St ☐ Coventry St

8. Dr Williams Library

☐ Gordon Square ☐ Woburn Square ☐ Mecklenburgh Square

9. Punch Tavern

☐ Covent Garden   ☐ Fleet St   ☐ King St

10. Gandhi Statue

☐ Montreal Place   ☐ Russell Square   ☐ Tavistock Square

SECTION 2

Question 1

Shown Below are 3 different routes between **Goring Hotel and The Wallace Collection**

Only 1 of the routes is correct. Place a tick in the box ☑ below the route you think is the **correct** one

Route 1		Route 2		Route 3	
Lve on L	Beeston Pl	Lve on L	Beeston Pl	Lve on L	Beeston Pl
R	Grosvenor Gdns	R	Grosvenor Gdns	R	Grosvenor Gdns
F	Grosvenor Pl	F	Grosvenor Pl	F	Grosvenor Pl
R	Knightsbridge	R	Hyde Park Corner	R	Knightsbridge
F	Hyde Park Corner	L	Park Lane	F	Hyde Park Corner
L	Park Lane	R	Stanhope Gate	L	Park Lane
R	Brook Gate	B\L	Deanery St	R	Brook Gate
F	Upper Brook St	L	South Audley St	F	Upper Brook St
Comply	Grosvenor Sq	Comply	Grosvenor Sq	L	North Audley St
Lve by	Duke St	Lve by	North Audley St	F	Orchard St
Comply	Manchester Sq	Comply	Manchester Sq	F	Portman Square
	S.D.O.L.		S.D.O.L.	F	Fitzhardinge St
				Comply	Manchester Square
					S.D.O.L.

☐   ☐   ☐

Question 2

Shown Below are 3 different routes between **Herne Hill Station and Trafalgar Rd, S.E.10**

Only 1 of the routes is correct. Place a tick in the box ☑ below the route you think is the **correct** one

Route 1

Direction	Road
Lve on L	Railton Rd
F	Herne Hill Junction
R	Dulwich Rd
R	Rymer St
L	Railton Rd
L	Hurst St
L	Dulwich Rd
F	Herne Hill Junction
F	Halfmoon Lane
F	Village St
Comply	Lordship Lane
Lve by	Gander Green
F	East Dulwich Grove
F	Nunhead Lane
F	Nunhead Green
F	Evelina Rd
R	Lausanne Rd
R	Queen's Rd
L	Kender St
R	Besson St
R+B\L	New Cross Rd
F	Deptford Broadway
F	Deptford Bridge
L	Greenwich High Rd
F	Greenwich Church St
R	College Approach
R	King William Walk
L	Romney Rd
F into	Trafalgar Rd

☐

Route 2

Direction	Road
Lve on L	Railton Rd
F	Herne Hill Junction
F	Norwood Rd
L	Croxted Rd
L	Turney Rd
L	Court Lane
B\L	Calton Ave
F	Townley Rd
R	East Dulwich Grove
L	Lordship Lane
Comply	Goose Green
Lve by	East Dulwich Rd
F	Nunhead Lane
F	Nunhead Green
F	Evelina Rd
R	Lausanne Rd
R	Queen's Rd
L	Kender St
R	Besson St
R+B\L	New Cross Rd
F	Deptford Broadway
F	Deptford Bridge
L	Greenwich High Rd
F	Greenwich Church St
R	College Approach
R	King William Walk
L	Romney Rd
F into	Trafalgar Rd

☐

Route 3

Direction	Road
Lve on L	Railton Rd
F	Herne Hill Junction
L by	Halfmoon Lane
F	Village Way
F	East Dulwich Grove
L	Lordship Lane
Comply	Goose Green
Lve by	East Dulwich Rd
F	Nunhead Lane
F	Nunhead Green
F	Evelina Rd
R	Lausanne Rd
R	Queen's Rd
L	Kender St
R	Besson St
R+B\L	New Cross Rd
F	Deptford Broadway
F	Deptford Bridge
L	Greenwich High Rd
F	Greenwich Church St
R	College Approach
R	King William Walk
L	Romney Rd
F into	Trafalgar Rd

☐

Question 3

Shown Below are 3 different routes between **Wilton Crescent and Vassall Rd, S.W.9.**
Only 1 of the routes is correct. Place a tick in the box ☑ below the route you think is the **correct** one

Route 1		Route 2		Route 3	
Lve by	Wilton Terrace	Lve by	Wilton Terrace	Lve by	Wilton Terrace
Comply	Belgrave Sq	Comply	Belgrave Sq	Comply	Belgrave Sq
Lve by	Upper Belgrave St	Lve by	Halkin St	Lve by	Chapel St
F	Eaton Sq	R	Grosvenor Place	R	Grosvenor Place
L	Hobart Pl	F	Lower Grosvenor Pl	F	Lower Grosvenor Pl
F	Lower Grosvenor Pl	F	Bressenden Pl	F	Bressenden Pl
F	Bressenden Pl	R	Victoria St		
R	Victoria St				
L	Vauxhall Bridge Rd	L	Vauxhall Bridge Rd	L	Vauxhall Bridge Rd
F	Bessborough Gdns	F	Bessborough Gdns	F	Bessborough Gdns
F	Vauxhall Bridge	F	Vauxhall Bridge	F	Vauxhall Bridge
F	Bridge Foot	F	Bridge Foot	F	Bridge Foot
F	Vauxhall Cross	F	Vauxhall Cross	F	Vauxhall Cross
F	Kennington Lane	F	Kennington Lane	F	Kennington Lane
R	Durham St	R	Durham St	R	Durham St
L	Harleyford Rd	L	Harleyford Rd	L	Harleyford Rd
F	Kennington Oval	F	Kennington Oval	F	Kennington Oval
F	Harleyford St	F	Harleyford St	F	Harleyford St
F	Camberwell New Rd	F	Camberwell New Rd	F	Camberwell New Rd
R	Foxley Rd	R	Foxley Rd	R	Foxley Rd
L or R	Vassall Rd	L or R	Vassall Rd	L or R	Vassall Rd
☐		☐		☐	

how2become

Question 4

Shown Below are 3 different routes between **Highbury Station and Queen's Square**
Only 1 of the routes is correct. Place a tick in the box ☑ below the route you think is the **correct** one

Route 1		Route 2		Route 3	
Lve on L	Holloway Rd	Lve on L	Holloway Rd	Lve on L	Holloway Rd
L	Furlong Rd	L	Furlong Rd	L	Furlong Rd
L	Liverpool Rd	L	Orelston Rd	L	Liverpool Rd
R	Offord Rd	L	Liverpool Rd	R	Tolpuddle St
L	Thornhill Rd	R	Offord Rd	L	Penton St
F	Barnsbury Rd	L	Thornhill Rd	F	Claremont Square
F	Penton St	F	Barnsbury Rd	F	Amwell St
F	Claremont Square	F	Penton St	F	Lloyd Baker St
F	Amwell St	R	Donegal St	R	Calthorpe St
R	Margery St	F	Rodney St	F	Guilford St
R	Calthorpe St	L	Penton Rise	F	Guilford Pl
L	Guilford St	F	King's Cross Rd	L	Lamb's Conduit St
F	Guilford Pl	F	Swinton St	F	Great Ormond St
L	Lamb's Conduit St	R	Gray's Inn Rd	R	Queen's Square
F	Great Ormond St	L	Guilford St	F into	
R	Queen's Square	R	Guilford Pl		
F into		L	Lamb's Conduit St		
		F	Great Ormond St		
		R	Queen's Square		
		F into			

☐   ☐   ☐

Question 5

Shown Below are 3 different routes between **Manor Fields** and **Bedford Hill**

Only 1 of the routes is correct. Place a tick in the box ☑ below the route you think is the **correct** one

Route 1

Lve on L	Putney Hill
R	Upper Richmond Rd
R	Keswick Rd
R	West Hill
L	Sutherland Grove
L	Granville Rd
R	Merton Rd
L	Kimber Rd
R	Garret Lane
L	Magdalen Rd
R	Openview
L	Burntwood Lane
F	Bellevue Rd
R	Wiseton Rd
L	Nottingham Rd
R	St. James's Drive
L	Sarsfeld Rd
R	Balham Park Rd
R	Balham High Rd
L	Balham Station Rd
L or R	Bedford Hill

☐

Route 2

Lve on L	Putney Hill
R	Lytton Grove
L	West Hill
R	Sutherland Grove
R	Granville Rd
L	Merton Rd
R	Kimber Rd
L	Garret Lane
R	Magdalen Rd
L	Trinity Rd
L	Nottingham Rd
L	St. James's Drive
R	Balham Park Rd
L	Balham High Rd
R	Balham Station Rd
L or R	Bedford Hill

☐

Route 3

Lve on L	Putney Hill
R	Lytton Grove
L	West Hill
R	Sutherland Grove
L	Granville Rd
R	Merton Rd
L	Kimber Rd
R	Garret Lane
L	Magdalen Rd
R	Openview
L	Burntwood Lane
R	Trinity Rd
L	Nottingham Rd
R	St. James's Drive
L	Sarsfeld Rd
R	Balham Park Rd
L	Balham High Rd
R	Balham Station Rd
L or R	Bedford Hill

☐

Question 6

Shown Below are 3 different routes between **Sussex Sq and Judd St**

Only 1 of the routes is correct. Place a tick in the box ☑ below the route you think is the **correct** one

Route 1		Route 2		Route 3	
Lve by	Stanhope Terrace	Lve by	Stanhope Terrace	Lve by	Stanhope Terrace
R	Strathearn Place	R	Strathearn Place	R	Strathearn Place
F	Hyde Park Square	F	Hyde Park Square	F	Hyde Park Square
L	Hyde Park St	L	Hyde Park St	L	Hyde Park St
R	Connaught St	R	Connaught St	R	Connaught St
L	Kendall St	F	Upper Berkeley St	R	Connaught Square
F	George St	F	Portman Square	F	Seymour St
L	Marylebone High St	F	Fitzhardinge St	F	Portman Square
R	Weymouth St	R	Seymour Mews	F	Wigmore St
L	Portland Place	L	Wigmore St	F	Cavendish Square
R	Park Crescent	F	Cavendish Square	F	Cavendish Place
R	Marylebone Rd	F	Cavendish Place	F	Mortimer St
F	Euston Rd	F	Mortimer St	F	Goodge St
R into	Judd St	F	Goodge St	L	Tottenham Court Rd
		L	Tottenham Court Rd	R	Torrington Place
		R	Chenies St	F	Byng Place
		R	Gower St	F	Gordon Square
		L	Montague Place	F	Tavistock Square
		Comply	Russell Square	F	Tavistock Place
		L by	Guilford St	L into	Judd St
		L	Brunswick Square		
		F	Hunter St		
		F into	Judd St		

☐   ☐   ☐

how2become

POINT SECTION ANSWERS

1. New King's Rd

2. Waterloo Rd

3. Belgrave Square

4. Parliament Square

5. Mile End Rd

6. Whitehall

7. Coventry St

8. Gordon Square

9. Fleet St

10. Tavistock Square

BLUE BOOK SECTION ANSWERS

1. 1   Correct
    2   "North Audley St" is a One Way St Southbound
    3   "North Audley St" is a One Way St Southbound

2. 1   "Village Way"; "Goose"; "East Dulwich Gr" & "East Dulwich Rd" are in the wrong order
    2   Correct
    3   No left turn form "Railton Rd"

3. 1   Correct
    2   "Halkin St" is a One Way westbound
    3   "Bressenden Pl" Left into "Vauxhall Bridge Rd"

4. 1   Correct
    2   Right "Swinton St"
    3   Right "Lloyd Baker St"

5. 1 Bad route
   2 Correct
   3 No right turn into "Trinity Rd"

6. 1 George St. no access to Marylebone High St
   2 No left turn into "Montague Place"
   3 Correct

AREA POINTS TEST

Time Limit: 12 minutes

During this test you will be required to answer questions based on the area of BARNES. Select your answer from the multiple-choice questions. You have 15 minutes to complete the test.

1. **Tree House Restaurant**

    ○ Castelnau

    ○ Church Road

    ○ Vine Road

    ○ White Hart Lane

2. **Barnes Sports Club**

    ○ Lonsdale Road

    ○ Queen Elizabeth Walk

    ○ Rocks Lane

    ○ Lowther Road

3. **Carmichael Court**

    ○ The Terrace

    ○ Grove Road

    ○ Castelnau

    ○ Ferry Road

4. Barnes Hospital

- ○ Morlake High Street
- ○ Lonsdale Road
- ○ South Worple Way
- ○ Mill Hill Road

5. Wetlands Centre

- ○ The Terrace
- ○ Lonsdale Road
- ○ Riverview Gardens
- ○ Queen Elizabeth Walk

6. Depot Restaurant

- ○ Washington Road
- ○ Barnes High Street
- ○ Castelnau
- ○ Tideway Yard

7. Sun Inn

- ○ Church Road
- ○ The Terrace
- ○ Barnes High Street
- ○ White Hart Lane

8. Mortlake Cemetery

- ○ South Worple Way
- ○ Verdun Road
- ○ Mortlake High Street
- ○ Mill Hill Road

9. Olympic Studios

- ○ Nassau Road
- ○ Station Road
- ○ Church Road
- ○ Glebe Road

10. Barnes Police Office

- ○ White Hart Lane
- ○ Barnes High Street
- ○ Station Road
- ○ Verdun Road

11. Swedish School

- ○ Suffolk Road
- ○ Lonsdale Road
- ○ Barnes Avenue
- ○ St Hildas Road

12. Bar Estilo

- ○ Vine Road
- ○ Station Road
- ○ Rocks Lane
- ○ Barnes High Street

ANSWERS TO AREA POINTS TEST

Question 1: Tree House Restaurant
Correct Answer: White Hart Lane

Question 2: Barnes Sports Club
Correct Answer: Lonsdale Road

Question 3: Carmichael Court
Correct Answer: Grove Road

Question 4: Barnes Hospital
Correct Answer: South Worple Way

Question 5: Wetlands Centre
Correct Answer: Queen Elizabeth Walk

Question 6: Depot Restaurant
Correct Answer: Tideway Yard

Question 7: Sun Inn
Correct Answer: Church Road

Question 8: Mortlake Cemetery
Correct Answer: South Worple Way

Question 9: Olympic Studios
Correct Answer: Church Road

Question 10: Barnes Police Office
Correct Answer: Station Road

Question 11: Swedish School
Correct Answer: Lonsdale Road

Question 12: Bar Estilo
Correct Answer: Rocks Lane

MAP TEST QUIZ 1

Time Limit: 10 minutes

You have 10 minutes to identify the locations on the map. This map relates to RUN 269 of the London Taxi Knowledge.

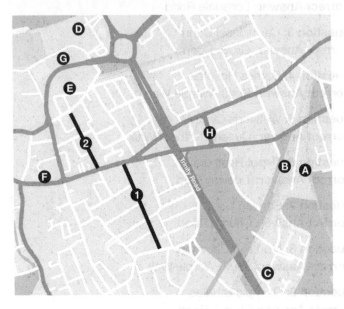

1. RUN 269 — Identify on the map the location of Emanuel School

    ○ A

    ○ B

    ○ C

    ○ F

    ○ G

2. RUN 269 — Identify on the map the location of the
    Clapham Rail Disaster Memorial

    ○ A

    ○ B

    ○ C

    ○ 1

    ○ 2

3. RUN 269 — Identify on the map the location of
    Geraldine Road

    ○ 1

    ○ 2

    ○ H

    ○ C

4. RUN 269 — Identify on the map the location of
    Wandsworth Town Hall

    ○ A

    ○ C

    ○ F

    ○ H

    ○ 1

5. RUN 269 — Identify on the map the location of Holiday Inn Express

    ○ C

    ○ D

    ○ E

    ○ F

    ○ G

6. RUN 269 — Identify on the map the location of The Ship PH

    ○ A

    ○ B

    ○ C

    ○ D

    ○ E

7. RUN 269 — Identify on the map the location of Tonsley Hill

    ○ 1

    ○ 2

    ○ H

    ○ C

8. RUN 269 — Identify on the map the location of Wandsworth Town Station

   ○ B

   ○ C

   ○ D

   ○ E

   ○ H

9. RUN 269 — Identify on the map the location of Marcilly Road

   ○ H

   ○ F

   ○ G

   ○ C

   ○ B

10. RUN 269 — Identify on the map the location of the Royal Victoria Patriotic Building

   ○ A

   ○ B

   ○ C

   ○ D

   ○ G

ANSWERS TO MAP TEST QUIZ 1

Question 1: RUN 269 — Identify on the map the location of Emanuel School
Correct Answer: A

Question 2: RUN 269 — Identify on the map the location of the Clapham Rail Disaster Memorial
Correct Answer: A

Question 3: RUN 269 — Identify on the map the location of Geraldine Road
Correct Answer: 1

Question 4: RUN 269 — Identify on the map the location of Wandsworth Town Hall
Correct Answer: F

Question 5: RUN 269 — Identify on the map the location of Holiday Inn Express
Correct Answer: G

Question 6: RUN 269 — Identify on the map the location of The Ship PH
Correct Answer: D

Question 7: RUN 269 — Identify on the map the location of Tonsley Hill
Correct Answer: 2

Question 8: RUN 269 — Identify on the map the location of Wandsworth Town Station
Correct Answer: E

Question 9: RUN 269 — Identify on the map the location of Marcilly Road
Correct Answer: H

Question 10: RUN 269 — Identify on the map the location of the Royal Victoria Patriotic Building
Correct Answer: C

MAP TEST QUIZ 2

Time Limit: 10 minutes

You have 10 minutes to identify the locations on the map. This map relates to RUN 269 of the London Taxi Knowledge.

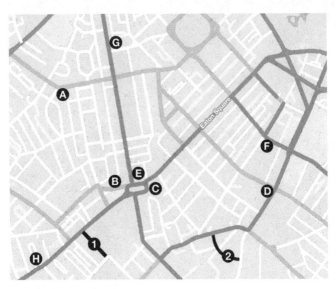

1. RUN 269 — Identify on the map the location of Victoria Coach Station

    O A

    O B

    O C

    O D

    O E

2. RUN 269 — Identify on the map the location of Markham Square

   ○ C

   ○ D

   ○ F

   ○ H

   ○ B

3. RUN 269 — Identify on the map the location of Boisdale Restaurant

   ○ H

   ○ F

   ○ G

   ○ B

   ○ E

4. RUN 269 — Identify on the map the location of the Heritage Lottery Fund

   ○ A

   ○ B

   ○ C

   ○ D

   ○ E

5. RUN 269 — Identify on the map the location of the Carlton Tower Hotel

    O C

    O D

    O E

    O F

    O G

6. RUN 269 — Identify on the map the location of Cheltenham Terrace

    O 1

    O 2

7. RUN 269 — Identify on the map the location of St Barnabas Street

    O 1

    O 2

8. RUN 269 — Identify on the map the location of Hellenic College

    O A

    O B

    O C

    O D

    O H

9. RUN 269 — Identify on the map the location of Moat House, Sloane Square

   ○ F

   ○ A

   ○ D

   ○ E

   ○ H

10. RUN 269 — Identify on the map the location of the General Trading Company

   ○ A

   ○ B

   ○ C

   ○ D

   ○ E

ANSWERS TO MAP TEST QUIZ 2

Question 1: RUN 269 — Identify on the map the location of Victoria Coach Station
Correct Answer: D

Question 2: RUN 269 — Identify on the map the location of Markham Square
Correct Answer: H

Question 3: RUN 269 — Identify on the map the location of Boisdale Restaurant
Correct Answer: F

Question 4: RUN 269 — Identify on the map the location of the Heritage Lottery Fund
Correct Answer: C

Question 5: RUN 269 — Identify on the map the location of the Carlton Tower Hotel
Correct Answer: G

Question 6: RUN 269 — Identify on the map the location of Cheltenham Terrace
Correct Answer: 1

Question 7: RUN 269 — Identify on the map the location of St Barnabas Street
Correct Answer: 2

Question 8: RUN 269 — Identify on the map the location of Hellenic College
Correct Answer: A

Question 9: RUN 269 — Identify on the map the location of Moat House, Sloane Square
Correct Answer: E

Question 10: RUN 269 — Identify on the map the location of the General Trading Company
Correct Answer: B

POINTS TEST — EMBASSIES

Time Limit: 5 minutes

Attempt the following 10 questions that relate to locations of Embassies in London. You have 5 minutes to complete the test.

1. Where is the High Commission for Pakistan?

    - ○ Queens Gate
    - ○ Princes Gate
    - ○ Lowndes Square
    - ○ Cadogan Place

2. Where is the Japanese Embassy?

    - ○ Piccadilly
    - ○ Pall Mall
    - ○ Park Lane
    - ○ Kensington Road

3. Where is the Chinese Embassy?

    - ○ Great Portland Street West side
    - ○ Portland Place West Side
    - ○ Great Portland Street East Side
    - ○ Portland Place East Side

4. Where is the French Embassy?

    ○ Princes Gate

    ○ Edinburgh Gate

    ○ Alexandra Gate

    ○ Albert Gate

5. Where is the Saudi Arabia Embassy?

    ○ Chapel Street

    ○ Belgrave Square

    ○ Charles Street

    ○ Curzon Street

6. Where is the Brazilian Embassy?

    ○ Green Street

    ○ Park Street

    ○ North Audley Street

    ○ South Audley Street

7. Where is the Cuban Embassy?

    ○ Hanover Square

    ○ Hanover Crescent

    ○ High Holborn

    ○ Holland Park

8. Where is the South Korean Embassy?

    - ○ Buckingham Palace Road
    - ○ Buckingham Gate
    - ○ Victoria Street
    - ○ Palace Street

9. Where is the Spanish Embassy?

    - ○ Belgrave Square
    - ○ Belgrave Place
    - ○ Chapel Street
    - ○ Chesham Place

10. Where is the Libyan Embassy?

    - ○ Knightsbridge
    - ○ Kensington Gore
    - ○ St James Square
    - ○ St James Street

ANSWERS TO POINTS TEST — EMBASSIES

Question 1: Where is the High Commission for Pakistan?
Correct Answer: Lowndes Square

Question 2: Where is the Japanese Embassy?
Correct Answer: Piccadilly

Question 3: Where is the Chinese Embassy?
Correct Answer: Portland Place West Side

Question 4: Where is the French Embassy?
Correct Answer: Albert Gate

Question 5: Where is the Saudi Arabia Embassy?
Correct Answer: Charles Street

Question 6: Where is the Brazilian Embassy?
Correct Answer: Green Street

Question 7: Where is the Cuban Embassy?
Correct Answer: High Holborn

Question 8: Where is the South Korean Embassy?
Correct Answer: Buckingham Gate

Question 9: Where is the Spanish Embassy?
Correct Answer: Chesham Place

Question 10: Where is the Libyan Embassy?
Correct Answer: Knightsbridge

POINTS TEST — HOSPITALS

Time Limit: 5 minutes

Attempt the following 10 questions that relate to locations of Hospitals in London. You have 5 minutes to complete the test.

1. Where is the London Chest Hospital?

    ○ Homerton Grove

    ○ Bonner Road

    ○ Old Ford Road

    ○ Sewardstone Road

2. Where is the Hospital for the Incurables?

    ○ Crown Dale

    ○ Knight's Hill

    ○ Crown Lane

    ○ Central Hill

3. Where is the Chelsea and Westminster Hospital?

    ○ Kings Road West of Beaufort Street

    ○ Kings Road East of Beaufort Street

    ○ Fulham Road East of Beaufort Street

    ○ Fulham Road West of Beaufort Street

4.   Where is the St Thomas's Hospital?

- ○ Lambeth Palace Road
- ○ Lambeth Road
- ○ Albert Embankment
- ○ Lambeth High Street

5.   Where is St Mary's Hospital?

- ○ North Wharf Road
- ○ South Wharf Road
- ○ Praed Street
- ○ Westbourne Grove

6.   Where is St George's Hospital?

- ○ Fountain Road
- ○ Blackshaw Road
- ○ Tooting Hill Road
- ○ Garratt Lane

7.   Where is the Highgate Private Hospital?

- ○ Denewood Road
- ○ Bishopswood Road
- ○ View Road
- ○ Bishops Avenue

8. Where is the London Clinic?

    ○ Marylebone Road

    ○ Harley Street

    ○ Upper Wimpole Place

    ○ Devonshire Place

9. Where is King's College A&E?

    ○ Denmark Hill West Side

    ○ Denmark Hill East Side

    ○ Caldecot Road

    ○ Bessemer Road

10. Where is St Charles Hospital?

    ○ St Marks Road

    ○ Barlby Road

    ○ Exmoor Street

    ○ St Quentin Ave

ANSWERS TO POINTS TEST — HOSPITALS

Question 1: Where is the London Chest Hospital?
Correct Answer: Bonner Road

Question 2: Where is the Hospital for the Incurables?
Correct Answer: Crown Lane

Question 3: Where is the Chelsea and Westminster Hospital?
Correct Answer: Fulham Road West of Beaufort Street

Question 4: Where is the St Thomas's Hospital?
Correct Answer: Lambeth Palace Road

Question 5: Where is St Mary's Hospital?
Correct Answer: South Wharf Road

Question 6: Where is St George's Hospital?
Correct Answer: Blackshaw Road

Question 7: Where is the Highgate Private Hospital?
Correct Answer: View Road

Question 8: Where is the London Clinic?
Correct Answer: Devonshire Place

Question 9: Where is King's College A&E?
Correct Answer: Denmark Hill West Side

Question 10: Where is St Charles Hospital?
Correct Answer: Exmoor Street

POINTS TEST — HOTELS

Time Limit: 5 minutes

Attempt the following 10 questions that relate to locations of Hotels in London. You have 5 minutes to complete the test.

1. Where is the Dorchester Hotel?

   ○ Park Lane

   ○ Piccadilly

   ○ Curzon Street

   ○ Deanery Street

2. Where is the Baglioni Hotel?

   ○ Kensington Gore

   ○ Kensington Road

   ○ Kensington High Street

   ○ Palace Gate

3. Where is the Millenium Knightsbridge Hotel?

   ○ Pavillion Road

   ○ Sloane Street

   ○ Sloane Avenue

   ○ Brompton Road

4. Where is the Landmark Hotel?

   ○ Lancaster Gate

   ○ Marylebone Road

   ○ Harewood Avenue

   ○ Langham Place

5. Where is the Ibis Hotel City?

   ○ City Road

   ○ Old Street

   ○ Commercial Street

   ○ Prescott Street

6. Where is the Berkeley Hotel?

   ○ Berkeley Square

   ○ Wilton Place

   ○ Farm Street

   ○ Berkeley Street

7. Where is the Guoman Tower Hotel?

   ○ East Smithfield

   ○ St Katherine's Way

   ○ Tower Hill

   ○ Tower Bridge Approach

8.   Where is the Westminster City Inn Hotel?

   ○ John Islip Street

   ○ Lupus Street

   ○ Victoria Street

   ○ Horseferry Road

9.   Where is the Hotel California?

   ○ Eagle Wharf

   ○ Crestfield Street

   ○ Belgrove Street

   ○ Belgrave Street

10. Where is the Hyde Park Towers Hotel?

   ○ Stanhope Terrace

   ○ Lancaster Terrace

   ○ Lancaster Gate

   ○ Inverness Terrace

ANSWERS TO POINTS TEST — HOTELS

Question 1: Where is the Dorchester Hotel?
Correct Answer: Deanery Street

Question 2: Where is the Baglioni Hotel?
Correct Answer: Kensington Road

Question 3: Where is the Millenium Knightsbridge Hotel?
Correct Answer: Pavillion Road

Question 4: Where is the Landmark Hotel?
Correct Answer: Marylebone Road

Question 5: Where is the Ibis Hotel City?
Correct Answer: Commercial Street

Question 6: Where is the Berkeley Hotel?
Correct Answer: Wilton Place

Question 7: Where is the Guoman Tower Hotel?
Correct Answer: St Katherine's Way

Question 8: Where is the Westminster City Inn Hotel?
Correct Answer: John Islip Street

Question 9: Where is the Hotel California?
Correct Answer: Belgrove Street

Question 10: Where is the Hyde Park Towers Hotel?
Correct Answer: Inverness Terrace

POINTS TEST — RAILWAY STATIONS

Time Limit: 5 minutes

Attempt the following 10 questions that relate to locations of Railway Stations in London. You have 5 minutes to complete the test.

1. Where do you set down for the Eurostar?

    ○ Midland Road East Side

    ○ Pancras Road East Side

    ○ Pancras Road West Side

    ○ Midland Road West Side

2. Where do you get the Stanstead Express in Central London?

    ○ Liverpool Street

    ○ Bishopsgate

    ○ Harwich Lane

    ○ Primrose Street

3. Where is Euston Station?

    ○ Euston Road

    ○ Eversholt Street

    ○ Melton Street

    ○ Euston Square

4. Where is Paddington Tube Station?

   ○ Departures Road

   ○ Praed Street

   ○ Eastbourne Terrace

   ○ Craven Road

5. Where is Nunhead Station?

   ○ Gibbon Road

   ○ Gibbon Street

   ○ Gibbon Lane

   ○ Gibbon Avenue

6. Where is Baron's Court Station?

   ○ Gibbon Road

   ○ Gibbon Street

   ○ Gibbon Lane

   ○ Gibbon Avenue

7. Where is Poplar DLR Station?

   ○ Baron's Court Road

   ○ Talgarth Road

   ○ Margravine Gardens

   ○ Gliddon Road

8. Where is Poplar DLR Station?

    - ○ Castor Lane
    - ○ Poplar High Street
    - ○ East India Dock Road
    - ○ Billingsgate Road

9. Where is Kensal Green Station?

    - ○ College Road
    - ○ Mortimer Road
    - ○ Hazel Road
    - ○ Harrow Road

10. Where is Golders Green Station?

    - ○ North End Road
    - ○ Golders Green Road
    - ○ Finchley Road
    - ○ North End Way

11. Where is Sydenham Hill Station?

    - ○ Sydenham Hill
    - ○ Sydenham Road
    - ○ College Road
    - ○ Dulwich Wood Park

ANSWERS TO POINTS TEST — RAILWAY STATIONS

Question 1: Where do you set down for the Eurostar?
Correct Answer: Pancras Road West Side

Question 2: Where do you get the Stanstead Express in Central London?
Correct Answer: Harwich Lane

Question 3: Where is Euston Station?
Correct Answer: Melton Street

Question 4: Where is Paddington Tube Station?
Correct Answer: Praed Street

Question 5: Where is Nunhead Station?
Correct Answer: Gibbon Street

Question 6: Where is Baron's Court Station?
Correct Answer: Gibbon Road

Question 7: Where is Poplar DLR Station?
Correct Answer: Gliddon Road

Question 8: Where is Poplar DLR Station?
Correct Answer: Castor Lane

Question 9: Where is Kensal Green Station?
Correct Answer: College Road

Question 10: Where is Golders Green Station?
Correct Answer: North End Road

Question 11: Where is Sydenham Hill Station?
Correct Answer: College Road

POINTS TEST — TOWN HALLS

Time Limit: 5 minutes

Attempt the following 10 questions that relate to locations of Town Halls in London. You have 5 minutes to complete the test.

1. Where is Shoreditch Town Hall?

    ○ Old Street South Side

    ○ Old Street North Side

    ○ City Road South Side

    ○ City Road North Side

2. Where is Camden Town Hall?

    ○ Crestfield Street

    ○ Argyle Street

    ○ Euston Road

    ○ Camden Street

3. Where is Kensington Town Hall?

    ○ Argyll Road

    ○ Campden Hill Road

    ○ Hornton Road

    ○ Hatherley Road

4. Where is Lambeth Town Hall?

    ○ Horsford Road

    ○ Acre Lane

    ○ Brixton Road

    ○ Brixton Hill

5. Where is Stoke Newington Old Town Hall?

    ○ Stoke Newington High Street

    ○ Albion Road

    ○ Vestry Road

    ○ Stoke Newington Church Street

6. Where is Westminster Council House?

    ○ Euston Road

    ○ Victoria Street

    ○ Westminster Street

    ○ Marylebone Road

7. Where is Southwark Town Hall?

    ○ Southwark Street

    ○ Peckham Road

    ○ Camberwell Church Street

    ○ Peckham High Street

8. Where is Hammersmith Town Hall?

   ○ King Street

   ○ Studland Street

   ○ Nigel Playfair Avenue

   ○ Dalling Road

9. Where is The Guildhall?

   ○ Aldermanbury

   ○ Cheapside

   ○ Gresham Street

   ○ Lothbury

10. Where is Tower Hamlets Town Hall?

    ○ Clove Crescent

    ○ East India Dock Road

    ○ Saffron Avenue

    ○ West India Dock Road

ANSWERS TO POINTS TEST — TOWN HALLS

Question 1: Where is Shoreditch Town Hall?
Correct Answer: Old Street South Side

Question 2: Where is Camden Town Hall?
Correct Answer: Argyle Street

Question 3: Where is Kensington Town Hall?
Correct Answer: Hornton Road

Question 4: Where is Lambeth Town Hall?
Correct Answer: Brixton Hill

Question 5: Where is Stoke Newington Old Town Hall?
Correct Answer: Stoke Newington Church Street

Question 6: Where is Westminster Council House?
Correct Answer: Marylebone Road

Question 7: Where is Southwark Town Hall?
Correct Answer: Peckham Road

Question 8: Where is Hammersmith Town Hall?
Correct Answer: Nigel Playfair Avenue

Question 9: Where is The Guildhall?
Correct Answer: Aldermanbury

Question 10: Where is Tower Hamlets Town Hall?
Correct Answer: Clove Crescent

POINTS TEST – PUBS AND BARS

Time Limit: 5 minutes

Question 1 — Where is Bradley's Spanish Bar?

- ○ Oxford Street
- ○ Charlotte Street
- ○ Hanway Street
- ○ Wardour Street

Question 2 — Where is the Island Queen Pub?

- ○ Noel Road
- ○ Curtain Road
- ○ Rotherhithe Street
- ○ Westferry Road

Question 3 — Where is The Fort Public House?

- ○ Southwark Park Road
- ○ Rotherhithe New Road
- ○ Old Kent Road
- ○ Grange Road

Question 4 — Where is The Polo Bar W1?

- ○ Hanover Street
- ○ Conduit Street
- ○ Bruton Street
- ○ New Bond Street

Question 5 — Where is The Dog Star Bar?

- ○ Railton Road
- ○ Coldharbour Lane
- ○ Brockley Road
- ○ Brockley Cross

Question 6 — Where is The Salt House Pub?

- ○ Salter Street
- ○ York Road
- ○ Wapping High Street
- ○ Abbey Road

Question 7 — Where is The Greenwich Union Pub?

- ○ Royal Hill
- ○ Creek Road
- ○ Trafalgar Road
- ○ Croom's Hill

Question 8 — Where is JuJu Bar?

- ○ Fulham Road
- ○ Old Brompton Road
- ○ Kings Road
- ○ Kensington High Street

Question 9 — Where is The Cantaloupe Bar?

- ○ Charlotte Road
- ○ Old Compton Street
- ○ Maiden Lane
- ○ Bedford Street

Question 10 — Where is The Pit Bar?

- ○ Southwark Street
- ○ Westminster Bridge Road
- ○ Waterloo Road
- ○ The Cut

ANSWERS TO POINTS TEST – PUBS AND BARS

Question 1: Where is Bradley's Spanish Bar?
Correct Answer: Hanway Street

Question 2: Where is the Island Queen Pub?
Correct Answer: Noel Road

Question 3: Where is The Fort Public House?
Correct Answer: Grange Road

Question 4: Where is The Polo Bar W1?
Correct Answer: Conduit Street

Question 5: Where is The Dog Star Bar?
Correct Answer: Coldharbour Lane

Question 6: Where is The Salt House Pub?
Correct Answer: Abbey Road

Question 7: Where is The Greenwich Union Pub?
Correct Answer: Royal Hill

Question 8: Where is JuJu Bar?
Correct Answer: Kings Road

Question 9: Where is The Cantaloupe Bar?
Correct Answer: Charlotte Road

Question 10: Where is The Pit Bar?
Correct Answer: Waterloo Road

POINTS TEST – POLICE STATIONS

Time Limit: 5 minutes

Question 1 — Where is Holborn Police Station?

- ◯ High Holborn
- ◯ Kingsway
- ◯ Lamb's Conduit Street
- ◯ Red Lion Square

Question 2 — Where is Streatham Police Station?

- ◯ Shrubbery Road
- ◯ Streatham High Road
- ◯ Stanthorpe Road
- ◯ Streatham Hill

Question 3 — Where is West End Central Police Station?

- ◯ Old Burlington Street
- ◯ Old Burlington Place
- ◯ Saville Row
- ◯ Cork Street

Question 4 — Where is Marylebone Police Station?

- ○ Seymour Place
- ○ Seymour Street
- ○ Marylebone High Street
- ○ George Street

Question 5 — Where is Rotherhithe Police Station?

- ○ Rotherhithe Old Road
- ○ Surrey Quays Road
- ○ Evelyn Road
- ○ Lower Road

Question 6 — Where is St John's Wood Police Station?

- ○ Allisten Road
- ○ Newcourt Street
- ○ Wellington Place
- ○ St John's Wood High Street

Question 7 — Where is Chelsea Police Station?

- ○ Fulham Road
- ○ New Kings Road
- ○ Petyward
- ○ Lucan Place

Question 8 — Where is New Scotland Yard?

- ○ Great Scotland Yard
- ○ Victoria Street
- ○ Horseferry Road
- ○ Broadway

Question 9 — Where is the Independent Police Complaints Commission?

- ○ Horseferry Road
- ○ High Holborn
- ○ Theobalds Road
- ○ Kingsway

Question 10 — Where is Harlesden Police Station?

- ○ Craven Park
- ○ Craven Park Road
- ○ Harlesden High Road
- ○ Manor Park Road

ANSWERS TO POINTS TEST – POLICE STATIONS

Question 1: Where is Holborn Police Station?
Correct Answer: Lamb's Conduit Street

Question 2: Where is Streatham Police Station?
Correct Answer: Shrubbery Road

Question 3: Where is West End Central Police Station?
Correct Answer: Saville Row

Question 4: Where is Marylebone Police Station?
Correct Answer: Seymour Street

Question 5: Where is Rotherhithe Police Station?
Correct Answer: Lower Road

Question 6: Where is St John's Wood Police Station?
Correct Answer: Newcourt Street

Question 7: Where is Chelsea Police Station?
Correct Answer: Lucan Place

Question 8: Where is New Scotland Yard?
Correct Answer: Broadway

Question 9: Where is the Independent Police Complaints Commission?
Correct Answer: High Holborn

Question 10: Where is Harlesden Police Station?
Correct Answer: Craven Park

POINTS TEST – SQUARES

Time Limit: 5 minutes

Question 1 — Where is Patriot Square?

- ○ Hackney Road
- ○ Cambridge Heath Road
- ○ Old Bethnal Green Road
- ○ Roman Road

Question 2 — Where is Red Square?

- ○ Carysfort Road
- ○ Red Lion Street
- ○ Highgate Hill
- ○ Green Lanes

Question 3 — Where is Northampton Square?

- ○ North End Road
- ○ New North Road
- ○ Spencer Street
- ○ Wyclif Street

Question 4 — Where is Chelsea Square?

○ Old Church Street

○ Sydney Street

○ Manresa Road

○ Beaufort Street

Question 5 — Where is Orange Square?

○ Victoria Street

○ Pimlico Road

○ Royal Hospital Road

○ Belgrave Road

Question 6 — Where is Warwick Square?

○ Belgrave Road

○ Rochester Row

○ Regency Street

○ Lupus Street

Question 7 — Where is Triton Square?

○ Euston Street

○ Robert Street

○ Warren Street

○ Drummond Street

Question 8 — Where is Vulcan Square?

- O Britannia Road

- O Manchester Road

- O Westferry Road

- O Preston's Road

Question 9 — Where is Nightingale Square?

- O Nightingale Lane

- O Wandsworth Road

- O Thurleigh Road

- O Endlesham Road

Question 10 — Where is Guinness Square?

- O Spa Road

- O Dublin Ave

- O Pages Walk

- O Abbey Street

ANSWERS TO POINTS TEST – SQUARES

Question1: Where is Patriot Square?
Correct Answer: Cambridge Heath Road

Question 2: Where is Red Square?
Correct Answer: Carysfort Road

Question 3: Where is Northampton Square?
Correct Answer: Wyclif Street

Question 4: Where is Chelsea Square?
Correct Answer: Manresa Road

Question 5: Where is Orange Square?
Correct Answer: Pimlico Road

Question 6: Where is Warwick Square?
Correct Answer: Belgrave Road

Question 7: Where is Triton Square?
Correct Answer: Drummond Street

Question 8: Where is Vulcan Square?
Correct Answer: Britannia Road

Question 9: Where is Nightingale Square?
Correct Answer: Endlesham Road

Question 10: Where is Guinness Square?
Correct Answer: Pages Walk

CHAPTER EIGHT

SAMPLE INTERVIEW QUESTIONS AND ANSWERS

Q. What should you check before taking your cab out?

A. You should check to see that it has a sealed taximeter, a fire extinguisher, up-to-date road tax and a certificate of insurance.

Q. How long is a taxi cab drivers license issued for?

A. 3 Years.

Q. What is the first thing you should do when you are issued with your license and copy of the license?

A. You should sign both of them.

Q. How do you know how many passengers a cab is licensed to carry?

A. On the back of the cab is the Hackney Carriage License Plate which will specify the number of maximum permitted passengers.

Q. Can anybody take your license from you?

A. Yes, only if a cab driver is supplying you with a cab.

Q. Do you need to wear a seat belt?

A. You do not need to wear a seat belt when plying for hire or carrying passengers However, you do need to wear a seatbelt when travelling to and from home you do need to wear a seat belt or if you are delivering a parcel.

Q. At the end of journey (carrying passengers) what should you check the cab for?

A. Make a thorough check to see that no property has been left behind.

Q. If you find lost property in a cab, what should you do?

A. No later than 24hrs after finding property in your cab you should got to any Metropolitan police Station, and get a receipt for the property.

Q. What is the minimum tread allowed on tyres (mm)?

A. The minimum amount of tread allowed is 1.6mm.

Q. Are remoulds allowed on a cab?

A. Yes, you can use remoulds providing they are P.C.O Approved.

Q. Why is the sliding partition restricted to only open 4.5 inches?

A. This is purely for the driver's safety.

Q. In an emergency, how would you stop a diesel engine?

A. By use of the cut-off switch.

Q. Where would you carry a wheelchair bound passenger?

A. You must always place them on the left of the driver, in the recess, facing towards the back.

Q. What should you do once a wheelchair has been placed in position?

A. You should make sure the brakes on the wheelchair are applied and that the restraining mechanism is used.

Q. What is the correct way to unload a wheelchair?

A. You should always unload wheelchairs using the ramps and always backwards from the cab.

Q. Are there any restrictions on what kind of cab a driver can drive?

A. Yes. However, if you passed your test in an automatic then you can only drive an automatic vehicle.

Q. What should you do if you are on a taxi rank and a vacancy occurs?

A. You must move up to fill the vacancies.

Q. If a notice of 'Unfit for Public Use' is issued on a cab that you are driving, what should you do?

A. You must stop working immediately and if the cab is being rented then you should return it to the garage and notify them. If you own the cab you must not use the cab until the repairs have been completed. Then you need to take it to the P.C.O for a check.

Q. If you are made aware that a passenger you have carried had a notifiable disease, what should you do?

A. You must report it to their local Medical Health Officer and get the cab disinfected before carrying any more passengers.

Q. What are the general rules when you are on a taxi rank?

A. No matter what part of the rank you are at, if you are plying for hire then you must be willing to be hired. Once you reach the front, the first two cabs must be available immediately.

Q. What items are you required to have on your possession when operating a cab?

A. When you take your cab out for work you must always have your badge (visibly on show). You should also have your normal driving license and your Taxi Cab driving license with you.

Q. If your cab catches fi re on a motorway, what should you do?

A. Pull over to the hard shoulder immediately and get your passengers out to a point of safety. Then, turn the engine off if this is possible. Use your fire extinguisher, and phone the emergency services if you cannot get it under control.

Q. Where would you find the engine cut-off switch on: (1) Fairway? (2) TX1? (3) Metro?

1. It is under the bonnet at the rear of the engine, on the left hand side

2. There is one behind the front number plate and one in the bottom right hand corner of the centre console.

3. One is located in the top right hand corner of the driver's compartment and there is also one just under the radiator grill (offside).

Q. What is the tyre pressure on:
(1) Fairway? (2) TX1? (3) Metro?

1. Front = 38psi — Rear = 36psi

2. Front = 35psi — Rear = 40psi

3. Front = 38psi — Rear = 38psi

Q. Are you allowed to have radial with cross ply tyres?

A. Whilst not advisable, you are permitted to have the same on one axle. You can have cross ply tyres on the front and radial's on the back.

CHAPTER NINE
USEFUL WEBSITES AND CONTACTS

Knowledge training courses
http://www.wizann.co.uk

Transport for London website
http://www.tfl.gov.uk/

Public Carriage Office
London Taxi and Private Hire
Palestra
4th Floor Green Zone
197 Blackfriars Road
London
SE1 8NJ

The PCO is open Monday to Friday (except Bank Holidays), between 08.00 and 16.00

 how2become

London taxi website
http://www.london-taxi.co.uk/

London taxi blog
http://london-taxi.taxiblog.co.uk/

Taxi sales
http://www.taxi-mart.co.uk/
http://www.elitelondontaxis.co.uk/

SOHO MAPS

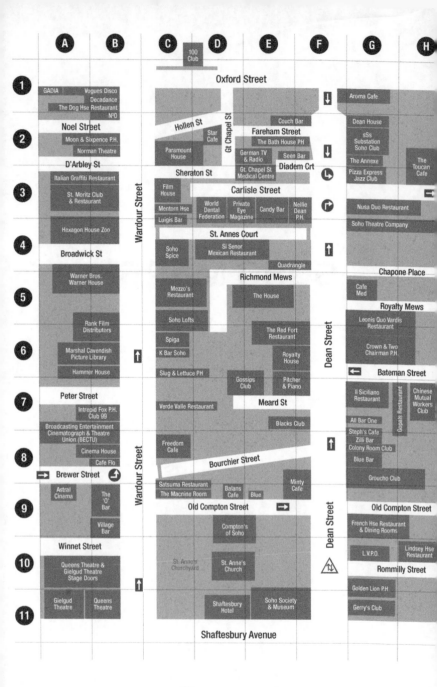

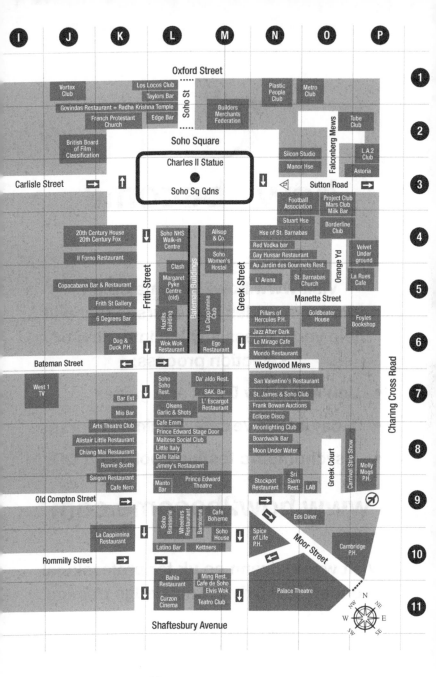